Based on the 'Winnie the Pooh' works by A.A. Milne and E.H. Shepard.

Published by Scholastic Australia in 2025.

Scholastic Australia Pty Limited
PO Box 579 Gosford NSW 2250
ABN 11 000 614 577
www.scholastic.com.au

Part of the Scholastic Group

Sydney • Auckland • New York • Toronto • London • Mexico City
Hong Kong • New Delhi • Buenos Aires • Puerto Rico

ISBN 978-1-76172-351-3

Printed in China.

Scholastic Australia's policy, in association with its printers, is to use papers that are renewable and made efficiently from wood grown in responsibly managed forests, so as to minimise its environmental footprint.

Disney

Winnie the Pooh: Caring For the Earth

SCHOLASTIC
SYDNEY AUCKLAND NEW YORK TORONTO LONDON MEXICO CITY
NEW DELHI HONG KONG BUENOS AIRES PUERTO RICO

‘Sometimes my footprints lead me round and round in circles, but I always seem to find my way home.’

It's up to us to find ways that we can keep and care for our home, the Earth, just like Winnie the Pooh and his friends treasure and appreciate the Hundred-Acre Wood.

As Winnie the Pooh says:

The world seems very bright and sunny,
When I start my day with hunny.
For then, I'm ready to explore,
No matter what I'm looking for.
The world outside holds much to see,
I cannot wait—tra-la, tra-lee!

Be More Green

'Did you hear?' Piglet asked Tigger. 'Pooh told me that Christopher Robin says that we're all supposed to be more green this year.'

'More green?' Tigger exclaimed. 'Why, I don't think tiggers are green at all! Whatever shall I do, hoo-hoo-hoo?'

He bounced off, feeling rather worried. When he ran into Eeyore, he told him what Piglet had said.

'Green, eh?' Eeyore sighed. 'It figures. Just when I'd come to terms with being a sort of dull greyish colour, everything changes.'

Eeyore told Rabbit what he'd heard. Rabbit shared it with Owl. Finally all of them came upon Christopher Robin and Pooh strolling in the Wood.

'Why, look at that!' Pooh said. 'Our friends are looking more green already!'

Going green is just a fun way of saying you're planning to be more mindful of your impact on the environment. Green = environmentally friendly.

Let's Make a Difference . . .

. . . by spreading the word!

What can one bear—or one kid—do to make a difference in the world?

Simple things you can do:

- Walk or ride a bike instead of going by car.
- Take a reusable bag to the store every time you go shopping.
- Sort the things that are recyclable (bottles, cans, glass, newspapers, metal, electronics, etc.) and put them in the proper recycling bin.

Skipping Stones

Nature delights us all through the year
With wonders to see, smell, touch and hear.
Its beauty we should always protect
By showing care, kindness and respect.

One sunny day on a walk to the pond, Pooh saw Tigger and Roo standing by the water.

'Hallo, Tigger,' said Pooh. 'Hallo, Roo. What are you doing?'

'Just a little exploritatin',' Tigger replied. 'After all, that's what tiggers do best!'

Looking down, Tigger noticed a green stone with yellow spots perched on the bank. 'How about we skip some stones, Pooh?' he asked. 'What do you say, Roo?'

Roo shouted, 'Yes!'

But Pooh was more hesitant. He knew how to skip, but doing it with stones was rather confusing. 'I suppose I could give it a try,' said Pooh.

Just then, Tigger picked up the large stone from the ground and held it in his paws. Suddenly, it began to rock back and forth and roll side to side.

'I've never seen stones move on their own,' said Pooh, shaking his head. 'Have you?'

'Don't be ridickerous,' Tigger said. 'Of course they can. How else do you think they skip?'

Just then, a green head, tail and four legs popped out. 'Yikes!' cried Tigger. 'Did you see that?'

He dropped the stone and the friends watched it crawl towards the water. 'There he goes!' cried Roo.

'It seems to me,' said Pooh, pointing to the creature, 'that what you have there is a turtle.'

'I knew that,' Tigger said. 'Tiggers love turtles. And do you know why?'

'No, why?' asked Pooh, shrugging his shoulders.

'Tell us!' said Roo. 'Please.'

'Well, buddy boys,' Tigger replied, 'The little fellas make tiggers look good, 'cause they always let us skip **faster!'**

Be a Scientist!

Pooh recognised a turtle when he saw one! You can be observant too—just like a scientist. Go outside and check out all the amazing colours of nature in your own backyard or neighbourhood.

Do you see any animals? Is there a squirrel gathering food? How does it hold an acorn? How does it climb a tree?

Do you see any birds? Are they flying overhead, splashing in a birdbath, or perched on a tree branch?

Maybe there's a cat or dog nearby, stretching, barking, meowing or running. See how they move. Listen to the sounds they make.

Look even more closely. Is something hiding in the grass or on a flower? Take a peek, but careful—don't scare the creatures away!

When you go inside, draw what you saw the animals and insects doing!

Feeding birds is a great way to watch them.
And it's as easy as saying,

'Let's make a birdhouse!'

You will need:

A milk carton
Acrylic paints
A paintbrush
Paper towels
A nail or screwdriver
String or wool
Scissors
A utility knife
Birdseed

Ask an adult for help.

- Have an adult cut out the sides of a clean, empty milk carton.
- Place the carton on a protected surface and paint with acrylic paints. Let it dry.
- Poke a hole into the top on each side of the carton with a nail or screwdriver.
- Thread a piece of wool or string through the carton and knot it at the top to hang.
- Fill with birdseed, find the perfect location outside to hang it, and be a bird-watcher!

Pooh Cleans Up!

Scrub and tidy,
Put things away,
Enjoy clean cupboards
For just one day.
It feels so good
When things are neat,
And when a friend stops by,
You can offer a seat!

Early one morning, Winnie the Pooh woke up, made his bed, got dressed and ate a rather large amount of honey for breakfast. 'Just the way I like to start my day,' said Pooh, feeling full and content. Then he looked around his house.

The cupboard doors were wide open and everything that was supposed to be on his shelves seemed to be somewhere else. 'Oh, bother,' said Pooh. 'It seems that I turned my house inside out looking for something. I wonder what it was.'

Pooh began to search all over again. He unmade his neatly made bed, throwing off the covers and pillow. Then he emptied his drawers, looked under the table and even removed the cushion on his favourite chair. Whatever he was searching for was nowhere to be found.

Pooh walked outside to his Thoughtful Spot. He sat on his log and began to think. 'What and where could it be?' he wondered.

In a little while, Piglet walked by. 'Hallo, Pooh,' said Piglet. 'Beautiful day, isn't it?'

'It is, Piglet, it is,' Pooh agreed. 'And it would be even more beautiful if I could think of just the thing that I'm trying to think of.'

'Oh dear,' said Piglet. 'I'm sure it will come to you, Pooh.'

Pooh wanted to invite his friend inside, but he realised that his house wasn't very tidy and he did not want Piglet to see the mess. Then he had an idea! If he put his things away, he could invite Piglet over for dinner.

'I'll see you later, Pooh,' said Piglet as he walked away. 'Yes, Piglet,' said Pooh. 'Come back and have dinner with me.'

And with that, Pooh went inside and swept and dusted and tidied and washed. Soon his little house was sparkling.

Piglet returned that evening carrying a basket of haycorn muffins and Christopher Robin's flashlight.

'That's it!' cried Pooh. 'Now I remember. I let you borrow Christopher Robin's flashlight. I completely forgot and I kept looking for it.'

'Oh, Pooh,' said Piglet. 'You gave it to me for my walk home one night.'

'I did indeed,' said Pooh. 'Well, at least it was a good reason to tidy up. I feel so much better since I did.'

Then the two friends sat down to a lovely dinner of haycorn muffins, vegetable stew (thanks to Rabbit's garden) and honey for dessert.

When it was time for Piglet to leave, Pooh turned to his friend and handed him the flashlight. 'Take this so you can find your way home.'

'Thanks, Pooh,' said Piglet. 'See you tomorrow.'

Let's Clean Up

Just like Pooh tidies his house, it's important to help keep the environment clean. You can do this by always putting your rubbish in a rubbish bin.

When you go to a park with friends, take recyclable bags and make a game out of picking up rubbish that you see. Make sure you're wearing protective clothing like work gloves and boots. Play a game to see who can fill their bag the fastest and fullest.

Green and Clean

For helping around the house, you can make an all-purpose cleaner out of safe, natural ingredients. Ask an adult to help you. Here's how!

What you'll need:

- Warm water
- White vinegar
- Fresh lemon juice
- Tea tree oil
- Safe essential oil like lavender or eucalyptus

Combine 1 cup warm water, 1 cup white vinegar, 4 tablespoons of fresh lemon juice and several drops of tea tree oil in a spray bottle. You can also add a few drops of an essential oil such as lavender or eucalyptus to balance out the smell of the vinegar. Shake to mix and use as a multipurpose cleaner.

A Dilly of a Day

'What a damp and rather dreary day, isn't it?' Christopher Robin remarked one rainy spring afternoon. 'Still, I suppose it's just as they say—April showers bring May flowers.'

'They say that, do they?' Pooh asked. 'But who is they? And when can we expect the flowers to arrive, exactly?'

He peered upwards, but he didn't see any flowers—just more rain.

Christopher Robin laughed. 'It's just a saying, Pooh Bear,' he said. 'You see, the rain falls in April, and that waters the seeds of all the wildflowers that have been lying dormant all winter. It reminds them to start to grow so that by May the Wood will be full of beautiful blooms.'

'Oh, I see!' Pooh said, looking up again at the rain falling down upon him. 'Thank you, raindrops. I do love flowers and so do the bees that make my honey!'

Weather and Climate

Weather and **climate**: these two words are related, but they don't mean exactly the same thing.

Weather is what's happening outside at the moment. In the winter, that means it might be cold or snowing. There could even be a blizzard! It's what your local TV forecast talks about every day.

Climate shows the bigger picture. It's the average of all weather in an area over many years. It takes into account the temperature range through all seasons, rainfall, wind and other factors.

Many scientists believe that the climate is changing throughout the world and that's one of the reasons for this book—to help kids learn how to help care for the Earth.

Piglet: Hey, Pooh, what goes up when the rain comes down?

Pooh: Why, I don't know, Piglet. What **does** go up when the rain comes down?

Piglet: An umbrella!

Let's Make a Difference

Collect rainwater to use in your garden or on your houseplants. It's safer for them than tap water, which might be treated with substances that aren't good for them. If you live in a house with downpipes, ask your parents to help you set up a barrel or some other container to collect the runoff. If you live in an apartment with a balcony, green space or rooftop, set out a bucket or tub to collect the rain that falls.

Keep a Weather Journal

Use a special notebook or a file on your computer to keep track of your local weather. You can note the date, the high and low temperatures and whether it was rainy, dry, windy, etc. After you've been doing it for a while, you can look back and try to figure out the weather patterns in your area.

Make a Weather Chart

Use construction paper and crayons or markers to make your own weather stickers: a sun, puffy clouds, dark clouds, rain clouds, snow, wind, etc. On a large sheet of white paper, draw and label a column for each day of the week. Now glue your stickers on each day to show the weather!

Christopher Robin: Pooh Bear, what's the difference between weather and climate?

Pooh: Think, think, think . . . I suppose I don't know, Christopher Robin. What *is* the difference?

Christopher Robin: You can't *weather* a tree—but you can *climate!*

The Seasons

We know that the seasons—winter, spring, summer and autumn—happen at different times of the year. And each season brings different weather. The changes happen because of the way the Earth orbits, or travels around, the sun.

In spring, the weather begins to get warmer and trees and other plants grow new leaves. Summer is the hottest season and has long, usually sunny days. In autumn, the weather becomes milder and leaves start falling from many types of trees. Winter is the coldest season, with short days. What's your favourite season?

Did You Know?

- Plants lose their leaves in autumn as the days get shorter.
- It's harder for animals to find food and water in the winter.
- Plants produce fruits and vegetables in their seasons.
- Some trees remain green in all four seasons.

Eeyore's Chilly Day

One very cold winter day, Pooh came upon Eeyore sitting on the riverbank.

'Is something wrong, Eeyore?' he asked.

Eeyore sighed. 'Do you mean generally, or right now in particular?'

Pooh scratched his head and thought over the question. 'Well, I suppose I mean right now,' he said after a while. 'That is, I can't help noticing you look rather gloomier than usual at the moment.'

'I suppose I am,' Eeyore replied. 'You see, I'm quite thirsty. But it's so cold that the river is frozen.'

'Oh, I see!' Pooh smiled. 'I think I can help with that, Eeyore.'

Pooh looked around until he found a stout branch. He used it to break the ice, revealing clean flowing water beneath.

'Thank you, Pooh.' Eeyore watched as a bird flew down to sip from the river, and then a squirrel scurried out to do the same. 'It seems I'm not the only one who was feeling thirsty.'

'You're very welcome, Eeyore.' Pooh smiled. 'I'm happy to help.'

Water in Winter

Winter can be a difficult time for wild animals and birds to survive. The number one thing that all living beings need is clean water. If you have a backyard with wildlife visitors, think about setting out a dish of water for them to drink when the weather gets cold.

Part of taking care of the planet includes taking care of you! Drink plenty of water and make sure you get enough sleep and a little exercise every day. That exercise doesn't have to be anything difficult—it can be as simple as going for a brisk walk outdoors, even in the winter.

Snow Candy

If it snows where you live, try making snow candy.

The only ingredients you need:

(1) A spot of clean, fresh snow
(2) Pure maple syrup

Ask an adult to help you heat the maple syrup to boiling, then pour it over your clean snow—and ta-da! **Snow candy!**

Snow Words

One cold winter day, Pooh was enjoying a smackerel at Rabbit's house with his friends. Suddenly Tigger bounced over to the window.

'It's flutter-shudder-flurryin' out!' Tigger cried.

'If you mean it's snowing, then you're right,' Rabbit said.

Pooh smiled. 'I like Tigger's words better. They sound so much more exciting!'

'Brrr!' Piglet exclaimed with a shiver. 'Sledding has been fun, but I'm getting cold.'

'Yes,' Christopher Robin agreed. 'Why don't you all come over for some hot cocoa?'

In Christopher Robin's dining room, Roo flung off his scarf, coat and sweater. 'Hey,' he said. 'It's cold in here too!'

Christopher Robin chuckled. 'That's because we're trying to save energy,' he explained. 'Heating a house takes a lot of it, you know.'

Kanga smiled and pulled Roo's sweater back on over his head. 'Surely we can all wear an extra layer in the winter,' she said. 'It's the least we can do to help the Earth.'

Pooh happily wrapped his scarf more snugly around himself, feeling a little warmer just from doing his part to help.

A Hot Topic

In places where it gets cold in the winter, home heating can use a lot of energy. Some of the most common types of heat, like gas and oil boilers or electric heaters, have the biggest, messiest carbon footprints. But the good news is people are always trying to invent newer, cleaner, greener ways of heating our homes, like solar, thermal, heat pumps and others.

Stay Warm Like Pooh

For those of us who live in an area where it gets cold in the winter, heating our homes is a necessity. But if it's safe for everyone in your family, ask your parents if you can turn down the heater a few degrees to save on energy use—and cosy up in warmer clothes around the house.

Tigger: Hey, Long Ears, what did one snowflake say to the other snowflake?

Rabbit: I don't know, Tigger. What did one snowflake say to the other snowflake?

Tigger: 'You're one of a kind!' Just like me, T-I-double-Guh-Rrr, Tigger!

Why Snow Matters

A fresh snowfall isn't just beautiful. Snow actually has a big impact on the climate! It's reflective and helps keep the Earth cool by reflecting sunlight instead of allowing it to be absorbed into the ground. Also, there are areas of the world where the majority of drinking water comes from snowmelt. Finally, certain species of animal, including the arctic fox and the ptarmigan, have evolved to camouflage themselves in the snow. Pretty cool, huh?

If you live where it snows, look for animals' tracks at the park or in your backyard. Take photos, try to figure out which animal or bird left each set of tracks and write down the results. It's amazing how many critters you'll find.

Winter Stars

'Oh, d-d-dear,' Piglet said with a shiver. 'It's already nearly dark!'

Pooh nodded wisely. 'I've noticed that this time of year, the sun seems much quicker to run away at night.'

'Yes and that makes the night much longer—and a bit scarier,' Piglet agreed.

'There's one good thing about the dark coming along so early, though,' Pooh said.

Piglet looked surprised. 'Is there, Pooh? What's that?'

Pooh sat down on his log and gazed up. 'It means the stars can come out while we're still awake!'

'Oh, I see!' Piglet sat beside Pooh. 'You're right, Pooh. And seeing the stars twinkling down on us makes the night feel much friendlier, doesn't it?'

Pooh smiled. 'It certainly does, Piglet.'

Stargazing

In many areas, the winter sky is ideal for stargazing. Cold air holds less moisture than warm air does, which makes the sky clearer. It also gets dark earlier, so you don't have to stay up as late to see the stars!

Let's Make a Difference

Light Pollution

Too much light at night can make it difficult or impossible to see the stars. It can also harm wildlife, including migrating birds. If you live in the city, there's probably not much you can do about outdoor light pollution. But if you live in the country or a smaller town, talk to your family and neighbours about turning off unnecessary outdoor lights earlier—or maybe not turning them on at all.

Early Spring

'Oh, my!' Piglet exclaimed to himself as he was crossing the Wood one chilly but pleasantly sunny day. 'I don't recall that meadow looking quite so alarmingly yellow yesterday.'

He paused, uncertain about whether it was a good idea to continue, as Piglet was a Very Small Animal and thus not always terribly brave. One of the things he'd learnt to be wary of was anything that changed abruptly from one day to the next.

Just then, Christopher Robin happened by. 'Oh, look, Piglet,' he exclaimed. 'The daffodils have finally begun to bloom!'

'The, er, daffy-what-now?' Piglet inquired politely.

'Daffodils,' Christopher Robin explained. 'They pop up every spring around this time. Aren't they beautiful?'

With his friend at his side, Piglet felt much braver. He followed Christopher Robin right over to the patch of yellow and saw dozens of lovely flowers.

'Oh,' Piglet said with relief. 'I see. Yes, beautiful indeed!'

All About Bulbs

Many popular spring flowers grow from bulbs. That means part of the plant—the **bulb**—stores food underground for much of the year. That's why you see them only at certain times. A daffodil might bloom for a few weeks; then its leaves remain above ground for another month or more, after which they disappear until the following spring. Some other popular flowering bulbs are tulips, lilies and hyacinths. Garlic and onions are bulbs too!

Corms (like crocuses or gladiolas), **rhizomes** (irises) and **tubers** (daylilies) are other types of storage systems similar to bulbs.

A Nature Journal

Remember that weather journal you read about on page 34? Why not add to your observations with a nature journal? Spring is a great time of year to start, since plants and animals are getting ready for the coming change in seasons. Write down the birds, insects and animals you see each day, along with anything interesting about their behaviour. Observe the plants and trees. Then write down any changes you notice.

Rabbit's Indoor Garden

One early spring day, Pooh stopped by Rabbit's house in search of a smackerel of something sweet. To his surprise, Rabbit answered the door.

'I was just about to get my gardening gloves and trowel, Pooh,' he said.

'But it's still rather cold outside, Rabbit,' Pooh said in surprise. 'Surely you can't work in your garden now.'

'Of course not, Pooh.' Rabbit led the way to the windowsill, where Pooh was surprised to see several bright green plants sprouting out of pots. 'I'm tending to my houseplants.'

'Oh, I see.' Pooh smiled. 'Since you can't garden out-of-doors, you've started a garden inside!'

Be a Gardener Like Rabbit

Having plants in the house is good for you! They can help improve your mood, increase creativity and maybe even keep the air a little cleaner. Plus they look beautiful!

Houseplants don't have to be plants you buy from the store. Try growing food . . . *from your food!*

You can collect the seeds from avocados or squash and grow a whole new plant.

Other foods can be grown from scraps, like sweet potatoes, celery, herbs and even pineapples!

You can also start your own little vegetable garden any time of year, right on your very own windowsill!

A pro tip from Rabbit: If you have pets or babies in your house, make sure the houseplants you choose aren't toxic, just in case someone decides to take a nibble.

Roo Wants Stew

Early one morning, Roo woke up and wanted to know what he and Kanga were going to do that day.

'Well,' said Kanga, 'it's warm and sunny outside. I think we should pay a visit to Rabbit's garden and pick the ingredients to make my summer stew.'

'What's a stew?' asked Roo.

'Oh,' said Kanga. 'It's a tasty dish made of all kinds of fresh vegetables and herbs.'

'Can I help make it?' asked Roo.

'Yes, of course,' said Kanga.

So after washing up and having breakfast, Kanga and Roo went to visit Rabbit's garden. Rabbit was already outside pulling vegetables and putting them in his wheelbarrow. 'I've been waiting for you, Roo,' said Rabbit. 'These vegetables are going home with you.'

'Oh, boy,' said Roo. 'But what are they?'

'Why,' said Rabbit, 'we've got radishes, beans, carrots, potatoes, onions, tomatoes, zucchini, yellow squash and celery. All the ingredients to make Kanga's summer stew. And it's going to taste especially delicious, because everything is grown right here in my very own garden!'

Just then, Roo saw Tigger. He called out to his friend.

'Look at these vegetables from Rabbit's garden. Mama and I are going to cook with them. And you can come over for dinner!'

'Those are some mighty colourful vegetabibbles!' said Tigger. 'And I betcha they're going to make one tiggerifically tasty stew—hoo-hoo-hoo!'

Buying Locally

Summer is the perfect time to visit a farmer's market for vegetables and fruits! You'll be helping your community by supporting the growers and you can learn more about how foods are produced. At the market, there will be fruits, vegetables, flowers, herbs and plants, grown and sourced right in your own town or area. You might even find Pooh's favourite—locally sourced honey!

Ask questions about the produce you see, like where it's grown and the difference between organic and conventional fruits and veggies. The people selling can even help you pick out the best-looking and ripest (most ready to eat) melons, strawberries, zucchini, tomatoes, etc.

Play "I spy" and search for as many different vegetables as you can! How many purple, green and yellow ones can you find?

Why not invent your own recipe, made to order for your particular taste buds? How about a yummy veggie omelette made with farm-fresh eggs? Or a ratatouille (kind of like Kanga's stew) with tomatoes, zucchini, eggplant and onions? Come up with a shopping list for your special dish!

Eating what you find at a farmer's market will make it taste extra special. After all, you selected the ingredients with your own two hands!

Bee-ing Helpful!

Where there's a farmer's market, there's sure to be honey made by Pooh's favourite insects—bees! As Pooh knows, bees are some of the most valuable creatures sharing our planet. In fact, they are responsible for almost one out of every three bites of food we eat. With that in mind, it's important to protect them.

Honeybees (Pooh's favourite!) live in large 'families' and can be found all over the world. The honeybee is the only social insect whose colony can survive many years. That's because they have a plan in winter. They huddle together and eat honey (like Pooh) when it's cold out and most flowers are dead.

Honeybees pollinate flowers and plants to feed themselves and help those plants grow. They are responsible for helping farmers' crops grow all over the world.

12 Un-bee-lievable Facts About Bees!

- Bees have five eyes and six legs.
- Honeybees live in hives (or colonies). The members of the hive are divided into three types: queen, workers and drones.
- There are more than 20,000 species of bees.

- Bees can see all colours except red. That and their sense of smell help them find the flowers they need to collect pollen.
- The average beehive can house around 50,000 bees.
- Each bee has 170 odorant receptors, which means they have a very powerful sense of smell.
- Worker bees go from one flower to another, collecting nectar. In one collection trip, a bee visits 50 to 100 flowers.
- Carpenter bees create tunnels that usually look about 5 centimetres deep, but they can be up to 3 metres long.
- The queen bee lays all the eggs in a colony. At the height of the season, she may lay over 2,500 eggs per day.

- Honeybees are great fliers. They fly at a speed of around 24 kilometres per hour and beat their wings 200 times per second.
- It takes 21 days for an egg to develop into an adult bee.
- Over the past 15 years, colonies of bees have been disappearing and the reason remains unknown. In some regions, up to 90 per cent of bees have disappeared.

Let's Make a Difference

The great thing about bees is that they're all around us! When taking a simple nature walk, try spotting a bee or two in your neighbourhood gardens. Watch as they move from flower to flower, gathering pollen and nectar as they go.

The Colours of Autumn

It was a bright, brisk, blustery day in the Hundred-Acre Wood. Piglet was pushed this way and that by the wind as he made his way to Pooh's house.

He was just about to knock when Pooh's door burst open. 'Hallo, Pooh,' said Piglet. 'Don't you think today is just the right sort of day for a ramble?'

'Oh, yes,' Pooh agreed. 'Let's go.'

The sky on this day was so blue, the colour so splendidly clear and true, that the two friends hadn't gone very far before they just had to stop and admire it.

'Have you ever happened to notice,' asked Pooh, 'how many different colours the sky can be?'

'Sometimes the sky is so dark, it looks purple,' said Piglet.

'Then there's that greyish colour when it rains,' said Pooh.

'And the colours the sky turns at sunset,' added Piglet. 'You can't forget those.'

The path the friends were following wound through a little meadow, where golden grasses made soft swishing sounds as the wind blew through them. Pooh and Piglet stopped to listen.

Shhhhhhhhh, said
the wind
in the grass.
Shhhhhhhhh.

'I would have been very sorry to miss that, Piglet,' said Pooh.

After some time, the path climbed a small hill, so Piglet and Pooh climbed it too.

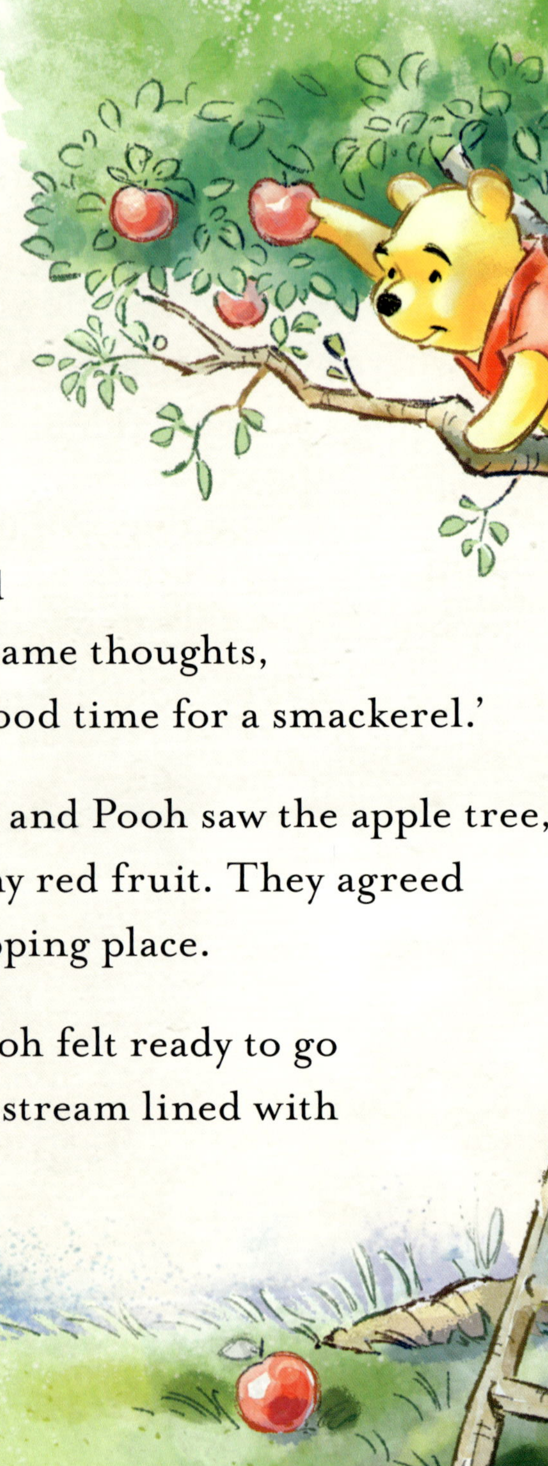

The wind carried the sharp, sweet scent of ripe apples, which filled Piglet's and Pooh's noses—and their minds—as they climbed.

'I was just thinking, Piglet,' said Pooh, whose mind and tummy very often had the same thoughts, 'that this would be a very good time for a smackerel.'

At the top of the hill, Piglet and Pooh saw the apple tree, its branches heavy with shiny red fruit. They agreed that this was a splendid stopping place.

In good time, Piglet and Pooh felt ready to go again. They soon came to a stream lined with trees in glorious autumn colours.

'It seems like just last week all the leaves were green,' Pooh said.

'I believe they were green last week, Pooh,' replied Piglet.

'I have always liked seeing the leaves change colour in autumn,' said Pooh. 'I think nature paints all the colours we really need.' He gazed up at the brilliant treetops.

'Yes,' added Piglet. 'I think so too.'

In autumn, tree leaves change colour, temperatures grow colder and plants stop making food. Animals have to prepare for the long months ahead. And even the days start getting shorter.

Fall Into Fun!

Ask an adult to rake backyard leaves into a big pile. Then you and your friends can take turns jumping into it!

Play follow-the-leader and lead your friends in, out and around a path lined with trees. Collect all the colourful leaves you can find!

Make a Wax Paper Leaf Print!

You will need:

- Leaves
- A large sheet of wax paper
- Colourful paints
- A large sheet of plain white paper

- Put your leaves down on a sheet of wax paper facing up.
- Cover the leaves with different colours of paint.
- Place the large sheet of plain white paper on top.
- Use your hand to press firmly across the paper.
- Remove the paper and voilà! You have a wax paper leaf print!

Piglet says:

Even though Pooh is tickled pink by nature,
he's still a sort of brownish colour.

Autumn breezes can send leaves—and Piglets—flying!

Pooh wonders:

Do leaves really know how to fly,
or do birds teach them?

The Three Rs

Reduce/Reuse/Recycle

Reduce, Reuse and Recycle Your Waste!

These are three great ways you can eliminate waste and protect your environment!

Think about all the things that we throw away—that is **waste.** It's stuff that doesn't get used. Waste, and how we handle it, affects our world's environment—your environment! The environment includes the air, water, land, plants and all man-made things.

For a healthy environment, managing waste is important. It has to be carefully controlled so it doesn't harm the environment and your health.

You can help by learning about the three Rs to manage waste: **reduce, reuse** and **recycle**! Practising all three of these activities every day is not only important for a healthy environment, but it can be fun too!

Candles and Honey

'Oh my, it's rather dark out,' Pooh remarked to himself one winter evening. 'Perhaps I'll light a candle.'

First he had to remember where he put them. As he looked in every cupboard and drawer, he found several honeypots but no candles.

'Hmmm,' said Pooh. 'I'm sure I put my candles somewhere for safekeeping, but where? Think, think, think!'

The only place left to look was under the bed. But as Pooh was a rather stout fellow, this would not be easy. Pooh took a deep breath in. 'Now, if I breathe out and pull in my tummy, I'm sure to be able to bend over and check.'

It worked. The candles were underneath his bed, alongside a jar of golden honey. He took the candles and jar over to his table. 'That was a tiny bit difficult,' said Pooh. 'I'll definitely need a smackerel to make me feel better.'

Pooh sat down, lit a candle and ate some honey. But it was still rather dark and he was still rather hungry. So he lit another candle and then ate some more honey.

And then he lit another candle and ate more honey. And did the same after that—several more times, in fact.

After a while, Christopher Robin stopped by. 'Is everything all right, Pooh Bear?' he asked. 'Your window is so bright I saw it from halfway across the Wood!'

It was only then that Pooh realised he'd lit all his candles and eaten all his honey.

'Oh, bother!' he said.

SANDERZ
RNIG

Saving Energy

We often do whatever we can to turn winter into summer, using a lot of energy to keep our homes very warm. Like Pooh lighting so many candles, we sometimes turn on every light in the house, even in rooms that no-one is using. (And sometimes outside too!)

But it's better to work with nature instead of against it. One way to do that is to think before, during and after using energy. Think, think, think like Pooh about whether you really need to turn night into day or winter into summer.

Let's Make a Difference

Remember to turn off the lights whenever you leave your room and unplug kitchen appliances that aren't being used, like the toaster. This is a small thing that can save a lot of energy over time. And it's so easy!

A "So-Much-to-Do" Day

Roo and his friends were spending a rainy day inside. When Roo asked his friends what they wanted to do, everyone shrugged.

When Roo looked around the room, he saw his and Kanga's things scattered about. There was an apron and kerchief hanging over a chair, a large box in the corner, a broom, Roo's paints and a basket filled with ribbons and wool.

'Let's see what we can make from things we find around the house,' said Roo excitedly. The friends joined in right away.

'Why don't you paint something on my apron?' said Kanga. 'That might brighten it up.'

And so they did. Then they made the box into a pirate ship and used the broom to hoist a flag made from Kanga's kerchief.

They hung ribbons on the walls to make colourful curtains and rolled wool into balls that they juggled and threw to each other for a fun game of catch. They even used the balls of wool for a game called "knock over the bottles".

By the time they were through, the sun was about to set. Kanga made a delicious supper. As they sat around the table, Roo and his friends could hardly contain their excitement.

'We turned a rainy, nothing-to-do day into a sunny, so-much-to-do day just like that!' said Roo.

'We did, indeed,' said Pooh, 'with just a little help from around the house!'

The Three R's

Christopher Robin was telling his friends about the three Rs: **reduce, reuse, recycle.**

'Recycle?' Tigger scratched his head. 'Is that something do with bibblecycling in the snow?'

'Not at all, Tigger,' Christopher Robin said with a smile. 'It's a way to lower our impact on the environment by making thoughtful choices.'

'I do like to reuse my honeypots by filling them with more honey,' Pooh remarked.

Christopher Robin patted Pooh on the head. 'Every little bit helps, Pooh Bear.'

Recycle

Recycling is when things that would otherwise be thrown away are turned into entirely new things. For instance, old newspapers can be turned into egg cartons, kitty litter, construction paper and all sorts of other things! Lots of materials are recyclable, from cardboard boxes to drink cans and many types of plastic containers. Products made of plastic are everywhere. Just think about all those plastic bottles! Try drinking water from a refillable bottle so you can avoid using a lot of plastic water bottles.

Be the Chief Recycler

If your family doesn't already recycle, why not volunteer to become the chief recycler at home? You can be in charge of reminding everyone to sort recyclable materials like paper, glass and certain types of plastics from the rubbish headed for a landfill. Ask a grown-up to check the recycling guidelines in your area and then follow them!

Pooh's Old Honeypot

It may be old or broken, it's true.
It may mean nothing at all to you.
But remember: There's more than one way to measure;
What you think is rubbish might be somebody's treasure.

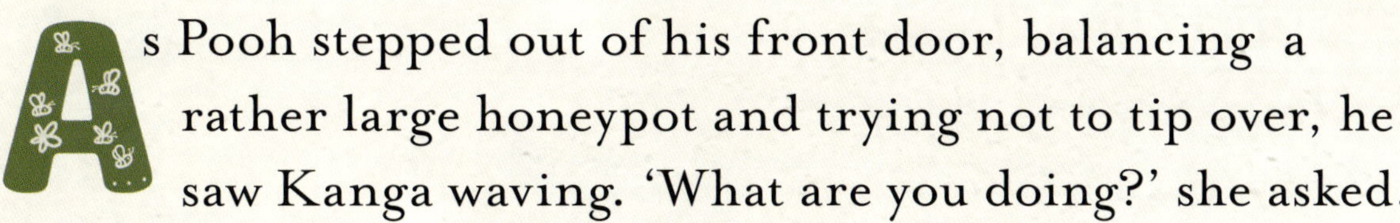

As Pooh stepped out of his front door, balancing a rather large honeypot and trying not to tip over, he saw Kanga waving. 'What are you doing?' she asked.

'I'm getting rid of this cracked, useless old thing,' said Pooh. 'A honeypot that won't hold honey is no good to me.'

'Oh, may I have it?' asked Kanga. 'I can use it as a planter for my spring flowers.'

'But it's cracked,' said Pooh.

'That's good,' Kanga replied. 'The cracks will let any extra water run out. That's just what a planter should do.'

Pooh waved until Kanga was out of sight. 'Who could have guessed that my Useless Old Pot would turn out to be Kanga's Perfect New Planter?' he asked himself. When no-one answered, Pooh shrugged. Some things were just meant to be mysteries.

What Pooh and Kanga did is called **upcycling!** Instead of throwing away an old toy or accessory, turn it into something new and useful!

Look! Pooh's honeypot became a pencil and paintbrush holder!

Outgrowing Your Clothes?

You're growing every day, which means you keep outgrowing your clothes. Just because they don't fit you anymore doesn't mean they can't be used and appreciated by others. Look how cosy Piglet is wearing Christopher Robin's old sweater! Some other kid might like your outgrown clothes just as much.

Let's Make a Difference

Ask your parents if you can sort through your clothes and find the ones you don't wear anymore. There are lots of organisations that help families who can't afford to buy new clothes. Ask your parents to help you find one near you so your old clothes can have a new life with someone else.

I'll Trade You. . .

Share, trade and exchange things instead of throwing them away. Have a toy swap with your friends! Somebody's old toy could be your new treasure.

How to Water a Tree

One lovely day in the Hundred-Acre Wood, Pooh went to visit his favourite tree. He noticed that the leaves were dry and crunchy and the branches drooped. Curious and just a bit worried, he went to Rabbit for advice.

'It seems to me the most logical reason is that your tree needs water, Pooh,' said Rabbit. 'But the trick will be how to water it.'

Pooh looked around Rabbit's house at all the pots, pitchers, bowls, tubs and watering cans lying about. 'Perhaps we could carry all these things to the tree and water it.'

'Good idea,' Rabbit agreed.

So they gathered their friends, along with all the pots, pitchers, bowls, tubs and watering cans, and headed into the Wood.

Since the tree was near the stream, they could fill all the pots and pitchers right there.

At the stream, Tigger borrowed one of the pitchers, filled it to the brim and spilled it when he took his first bounce.

And when Roo tried to pull a large tub out of the water and onto the bank, he fell into the stream and spilled all the water.

'No, no!' scolded Rabbit. 'We don't want to do that.'

'I have an idea,' said Kanga as she fished Roo out of the stream. 'Why don't we all do what we do best? Eeyore is quite strong, so he can pull the containers out of the stream. And the rest of us can form a line from the stream to the tree and pass the water along.'

So on that day, and every hot, dry day from then on, the friends all came together and watered Pooh's favourite tree. Soon it began to look green and splendid again.

Then one day, something changed, and that something was the weather. The sky turned from blue to grey and the wind began to blow.

'Must be Tigger splashing us,' said Eeyore as a drop of water hit him.

'I think the sky is splashing us,' said Pooh, looking up just as a rather large raindrop landed on his nose.

The friends ran to Pooh's favourite tree. They stood together under the tree's big, sheltering branches and they cheered—for the rain and the tree and each other.

Saving Water

Water **conservation** means using water thoughtfully so we do not waste it. Using less water is important because fresh, clean water is a limited resource, as well as a costly one.

We need to save water so we will have enough to keep our bodies healthy, to grow the food that we eat and to preserve natural habitats.

Let's Make a Difference

Calculate your water footprint. You probably have no idea how many gallons of water you need to take a bath or a shower, wash clothes or brush your teeth. Watch what you're doing and be mindful so you don't let the water run and waste it! Bath or shower? Try a bath and see if you use less water.

If you like showers, who in your family can take the shortest one? Then see who can collect the most water to reuse for watering the garden. Who can fit the most dishes in the dishwasher while still leaving plenty of room for the soap to do its job? Did you know that one load of laundry can use around 25 gallons of water?

Be a Leak Detective

The main source of water waste in your home could be going unnoticed! Leaky faucets, running toilets, broken sprinklers—whatever it is, keep an eye out for these little things by being a **leak detective.** From listening for drips to looking for places that never dry, playing detective is a fun way to help you train your senses and tune in to your environment.

Water-Wise Gardening

Finally, if you love being outdoors, one of the best ways to get thinking about conserving water is to help in the design and upkeep of a garden. For starters, you can help place bins and gauges to track and collect rainwater for watering the plants. You can even find places in the yard where water naturally gathers during rainy days and then plant vegetation that will use that water rather than let it run or evaporate away (these are called **rain gardens**).

If you don't live in an area where you get enough rain for a rain garden, pick out some drought-tolerant plants that can survive and thrive until the next sprinkle of reused or collected water. You'll enjoy feeling responsible and proud when it comes to taking care of plants that you chose yourself!

Piglet's Butterfly Blues

One day, Piglet was out looking for butterflies. He looked everywhere in the Wood, but he couldn't find a single one. So Piglet went to visit Winnie the Pooh.

'Hallo, Piglet,' said Pooh. 'Won't you come in?'

'No, thank you, Pooh,' said Piglet, 'but I'm hoping you'll come with me to find some butterflies. I've looked everywhere and I don't see any.'

'Of course I'll help you,' said Pooh.

So the two friends walked and searched and searched and walked quite a ways. Soon they came upon Rabbit's garden. And there, among Rabbit's flowers and plants, were bunches of bright, colourful butterflies fluttering in the breeze while hovering above the flowers.

'How clever of these butterflies to be in Rabbit's garden,' said Piglet. 'They must like to eat the things that grow here as much as we do.'

'Imagine that!' Pooh said. 'I had no idea that butterflies' tummies get rumbly just like mine.'

Nothing Better Than Butterflies

Everybody loves beautiful butterflies. These insects visit flowering plants and drink their nectar. While the butterfly is feeding, tiny pollen grains (like powder) will often stick to the insect's legs or body. As the butterfly travels from plant to plant, the grains get dropped off.

Receiving other plants' pollen allows a plant to reproduce and grow seeds. This helps the plants, as well as all the people and animals that eat the fruits and vegetables these plants make. Foods that rely on pollination include apples, blueberries, chocolate, vanilla, peaches and potatoes.

Monarch Butterflies

Like all living things, butterflies need water, food and habitat. In addition, **monarch** butterflies depend on milkweed—a grassland plant that provides them with a place to lay their eggs and a source of food for their baby caterpillars.

As grasslands become fields of corn, wheat or other crops used to feed people, milkweed and other plants are disappearing. The plants disappear under plows or get covered in herbicides so that they don't interfere with the growing crops. If monarchs lose these plants, they won't be around to pollinate and help produce our fruits and vegetables.

Go Native!

Native plants matter. Native plants are plants that grow naturally in a place. They are important because they help keep the environment healthy. Native plants provide food and homes for animals like birds, bees and butterflies. They also help keep the soil strong and clean the air we breathe. By growing native plants, we can make sure our world stays beautiful and healthy for everyone.

To learn about the native plants in your area, ask an adult to help you look online or visit the library for books about local plants. You can also visit a nearby nature centre and talk to a local nature expert. Once you know which plants are native to your neighbourhood, you can get seeds or small plants from a garden store and plant them in your garden.

One "Crunchity" Carrot

One day, Pooh and Tigger walked by Rabbit's garden and saw him pushing a wheelbarrow filled with old rotting fruits and vegetables.

'Hey, Long Ears,' called Tigger. 'Whatcha doin' with that there smelly stuff?'

'Oh dear,' said Pooh. 'I hope you're not working on a new recipe. Those ingredients do look rather strange.'

'If he is, we're not staying for lunch, Buddy Boy!' called Tigger.

'Well,' said Rabbit, 'if you must know, I'm starting a composting pile.'

'A compositatin'—uh—hmmm—what kind of pile?' asked Tigger.

'A composting pile,' Rabbit repeated. 'I mix these old food scraps with dry leaves, twigs, grass, eggshells, et cetera. And, in a while, it all breaks down into a healthy, rich soil that goes back into feeding my garden.'

'It all sounds kinda compostposterous to me,' Tigger said, bouncing up and down.

'Oh, really?' Rabbit said, pulling a long orange carrot from his basket. He handed it to Tigger. 'Well, just taste this!'

'Hoo-hoo-hoo!' cried Tigger. 'That's one crunchity carrot! And it's compostitively delicious!'

Composting Like Rabbit!

Compost is a nutrient-rich soil that is created when organic materials like leaves, grass clippings and food scraps decompose (or break down) naturally. By creating a composting bin in your backyard, you're trapping helpful microorganisms within this pile of organic material and speeding up the process.

Adding compost to a garden enriches the soil with nutrients that help fruits, vegetables and flowers grow. Composting can lead to healthier vegetables and fruits for meals.

Remember the three Rs? By composting, you **reduce** the amount of garbage you throw out, you **reuse** the materials and you **recycle** the nutrients back into the soil.

The easiest way is to use a compost bin and let nature take its course. Dump your organic, or natural, waste in the compost bin and wait. Depending on the size and type of the scraps, it will take between three to six months to produce good, healthy compost. The bin keeps it contained as you keep adding to it.

Let's Make a Compost Pile

- Select your materials. Start with food scraps from fruits and veggies—the skin of a sweet potato, the top of your strawberry. Also tea bags, coffee grounds, eggshells, old flowers—even human hair!
- Store those organic scraps.
- Choose a place to make your compost.
- Make the compost mix.
- Wait and let it breathe.

Curious Like Pooh

Early one sunny spring day, Pooh and Piglet were walking in the Wood when they came upon a soft rustling sound. Now, Piglet's ears worked very well and he could hear the sound as the two friends approached.

Being rather timid and always on the watch for heffalumps and woozles, Piglet quickly ducked behind a very large tree and refused to come out.

Pooh, on the other hand, was rather curious. He tried coaxing his friend. 'Piglet,' Pooh began. 'I'm quite sure there aren't any heffalumps or woozles about. So we may just want to see what's making that noise.'

'Oh, good idea, Pooh,' said Piglet. 'Go right ahead.'

'Well,' said Pooh, 'just in case it's a baby bird out of its nest, perhaps you should look with me.'

'Very well,' Piglet said nervously. 'But you go first.'

So with Pooh in front and Piglet behind, the two friends gently poked at the clump of grass and leaves that was making the sound.

And when they did, a little black nose poked out from beneath. It was a baby fox.

'I think she's smiling at me,' said Piglet, feeling relieved.

'Of course she is,' said Pooh. 'You are very brave.'

The two watched as the baby fox jumped up and ran back to her den.

'I guess she's curious like you, Pooh,' said Piglet. 'It would have been a shame to have missed her. It's good to know that some wild animals are not what we might think of as wild.'

'And then, of course, there's Tigger,' said Pooh with a rather large grin on his face.

Eeyore's Special Tree

One hot summer day, Pooh and his friends were enjoying the shade of a rather large tree in the Hundred-Acre Wood.

'Remind me again why we love this tree so much,' said Pooh.

'I like to sit in the tip-top branches of this very tree and watch the sunrise,' said Owl. 'It's a particularly fine place to think about the bigness and smallness of things.'

'And this is the tree where I learned to swing!' said Roo.

'I used to bring him to this tree when he was just a wee Roo,' said Kanga. 'The branches are so sturdy and strong. I trusted this tree to hold up my adorable Roo.'

'And I happen to know that this here tree has the crunchiest leaves in the whole Hundred-Acre Wood!' said Tigger.

Just then, Eeyore arrived.

Piglet gasped; Pooh gulped.

'Eeyore,' said Rabbit. 'You have a tree growing out of your back.'

Eeyore looked over his shoulder. 'It's not growing there,' he said. 'I'm just giving it a ride. I thought I would plant it here.'

Eeyore pointed to a sunny spot next to everyone's favourite tree. 'You see, every spring this tree is covered with sweet-smelling blossoms. It always makes me feel, well, nearly cheerful. When I saw that the big tree looked lonely, I wanted to cheer it up. So I brought a little tree to keep it company.'

'Everyone feels better when they have a little company,' Pooh agreed.

Then Eeyore's friends—all of them together—helped him plant the little tree.

Let's Talk Trees!

Roo: Hey, Pooh, what's a tree's least favourite month of the year?

Pooh: I don't know, Roo. What's a tree's least favourite month of the year?

Roo: Sep-timber!

These are two kinds of trees that you might find in your local park—depending on where you live, of course!

Coniferous Trees

These are trees that produce cones as seeds. The seeds are normally called **pinecones,** but not all coniferous trees are pine trees! Coniferous trees have needles instead of leaves and will retain many of them during the winter. If you look at a variety of coniferous trees, you will see that pinecones come in all kinds of shapes and sizes, and the branches of these trees have different-shaped needles and different smells.

Deciduous Trees

These are trees that lose their leaves in the winter. **Oak, maple** and **elm** are all examples. These trees usually have leaves that change colour in autumn.

Go on a Tree Scavenger Hunt

Nature hunts can be tons of fun. Try a tree scavenger hunt. Look for different kinds of trees and pick up **leaves, pods, seeds** and **cones.** Start your very own collection!

Use your natural materials to make a cool collage! Construction paper, glue, leaves, seeds and pods should do the trick!

Be a Tree Hugger Like Pooh

Pooh knows that trees are important—especially a certain honey tree! But there's more to trees than just bees. They're amazing from bottom to top! Their roots help hold the soil in place to prevent runoffs and flooding and their branches and leaves create shade and help regulate the temperature. They also provide habitats for lots of animals, birds and insects. They're such an incredibly important part of the world's ecosystems that it's no wonder that environmentalists are sometimes called tree huggers!

If all this whets your appetite for trees, you can make a sweet and salty tree snack for yourself. Just get pretzel rods (for the trunk), pretzel sticks (for the branches) and green grapes cut in half (for the leafy top) and design your own tasty tree! **Tree-licious!**

Let's Make a Difference

Just like Eeyore, plant a tree! Any kind will do, though native species (trees that naturally live in your area) are best. Look up what your tree needs to thrive, whether that's full sun, wet soil or a spot out of the wind. Then plant it in a suitable spot, keep it watered until it settles in and watch it grow taller from year to year. You can even hug it if you want to!

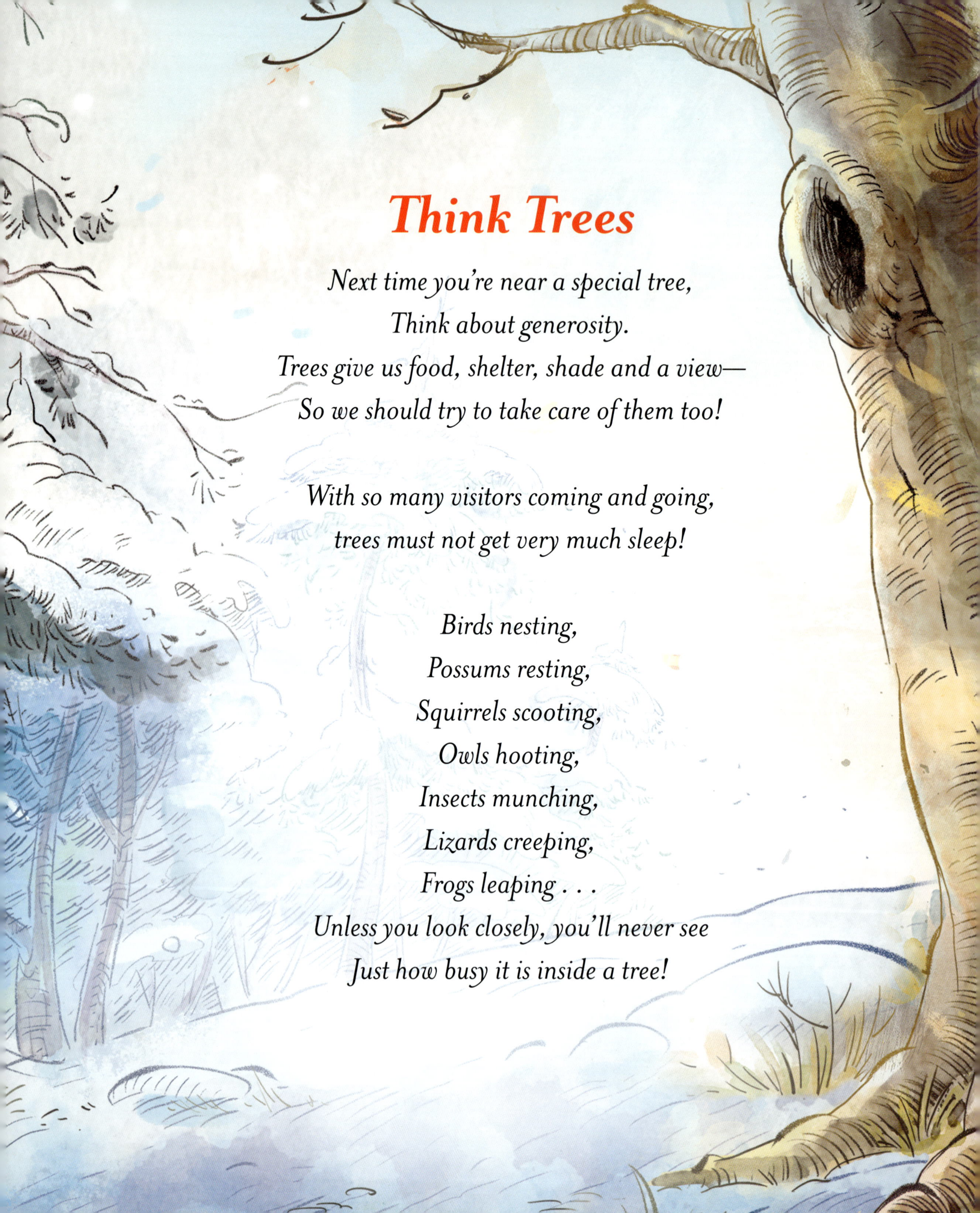

Think Trees

Next time you're near a special tree,
Think about generosity.
Trees give us food, shelter, shade and a view—
So we should try to take care of them too!

With so many visitors coming and going,
trees must not get very much sleep!

Birds nesting,
Possums resting,
Squirrels scooting,
Owls hooting,
Insects munching,
Lizards creeping,
Frogs leaping . . .
Unless you look closely, you'll never see
Just how busy it is inside a tree!

Thank You, Tree

Thank you, tree,
For cooling shade
And lemons to make
lemonade.
For haycorns and
Their handy caps,
For comfy trunks
Where Pooh Bear naps.

We're grateful for
All this, it's true,
But what we love
Most about you
Is that wherever
We may roam,
You're always here
When we come home!

When Pooh and his friends think about their home in the Hundred-Acre Wood, they are grateful that it's safe, protected and clean. Keeping it that way means picking up after themselves after they've been picnicking and partying in the Wood.

Think about how you clean up after yourself when you've been to a friend's house! It's important to show the same respect and courtesy everywhere you go—especially when you're out in nature. After visiting a beach, campground, park, garden or forest, don't leave bottles, papers or anything else lying about. Even if you have to walk a ways to find a rubbish bin, you can gather all the waste into a bag and discard it when you find the proper container.

'Listen!' shouted Tigger from inside a cave. 'I love to hear my "hoo-hoo-hoo" echoing out loud!'

'Perhaps you shouldn't shout,' warned Piglet. 'You wouldn't want to wake any creatures that might be taking a little nap in here.'

Piglet is right! Have respect for the wildlife you encounter in nature. This is their home. And if you don't like screaming and shouting in your house, why would animals like it in theirs?

Pay attention to signs and follow them. If you see a "no trespassing" sign, do not enter. Some areas in a park, forest, botanical garden or beach setting might be protected. And if you are in a place that allows campfires, make sure any fire you build is completely out before you leave. Don't leave any smoking embers behind!

Be mindful where you walk and what you touch! You wouldn't want to hurt any plant life or flowers by stepping on them or picking them.

Pooh's Walkabout

Whenever I'm feeling especially stout
I find it feels fine to go walking about
Ho, ho, ho
To and fro!
When I become weary with legs feeling funny
I'll stop at a friend's for a smackerel of honey
Yum, yum, yum
Hum, hum, hum
Now my walkabout is done!

Make Every Day Earth Day

Here's a list of things to remember when you're thinking about caring for and keeping the Earth! You'll feel like a great green hero when you do!

- Go Green
- Pick Up Litter
- Turn Out the Lights
- Save Energy
- Reduce, Reuse, Recycle
- Conserve Water
- Buy Locally Sourced Produce
- Compost Food Waste
- Protect and Respect Wild Animals
- Plant a Tree

Tigger: Hoo-hoo-hoo! You're doing a splendiferous job caring for and keeping the Earth!

Pooh: And my friends and I say thank you!

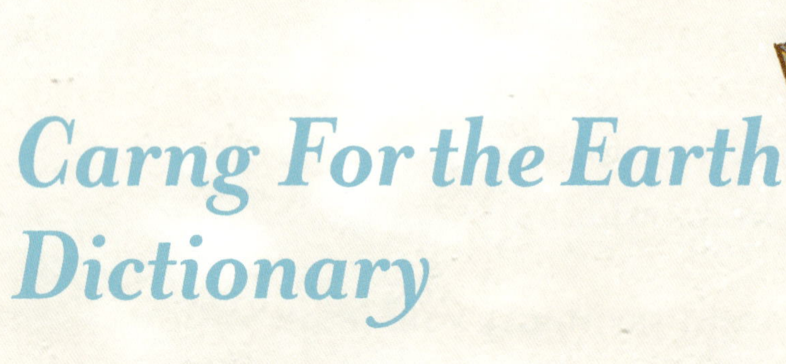

Carng For the Earth Dictionary

Compost: Compost is a mix of old food scraps and plants that breaks down into soil. It's used to help new plants grow.

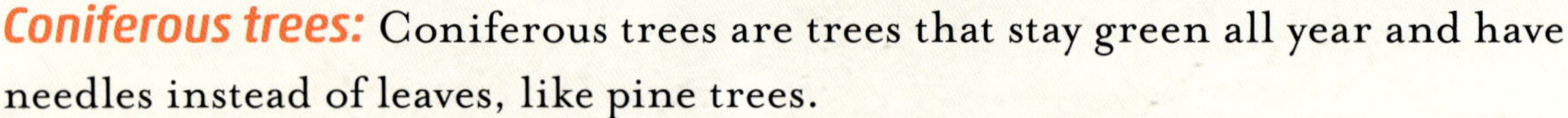

Coniferous trees: Coniferous trees are trees that stay green all year and have needles instead of leaves, like pine trees.

Deciduous trees: Deciduous trees are trees that lose their leaves every autumn and grow new ones in the spring, like oak or maple trees.

Endangered species: Endangered species are animals or plants that are at risk of disappearing forever because there aren't many of them left.

Environmental footprint: An environmental footprint is how much we affect the Earth by using resources like water or energy, or even by producing waste.

Going green: Going green means making choices to help protect and preserve the planet, like recycling or using less electricity.

Light pollution: Light pollution is when there is too much man-made light, like from street lights, which can make it hard to see the stars at night.

Organic foods: Organic foods are grown without using chemicals, like pesticides or fertilisers, that can harm the environment.

Water conservation: Water conservation means saving water and using it wisely so we don't waste this important resource.

Disney
Winnie the Pooh
Caring For the Earth
Certificate of Achievement
For practising environmental good works!
©Disney

SANDERS